IDEAS AND INVENTIONS

SEA, SKY AND SPACE

Transport Technology on Earth and in Space

Philip Wilkinson

Illustrated by Robert Ingpen

Chrysalis Children's Books

First published in the UK in 2005 by
Chrysalis Children's Books
An imprint of Chrysalis Books Group Plc,
The Chrysalis Building, Bramley Road, London W10 6SP

ISBN   1 84458 216 7

British Library Cataloguing in Publication Data
for this book is available from the British Library.

Editorial Manager: Joyce Bentley
Senior Editor: Rasha Elsaeed
Series Editor: Jon Richards
Editorial Assistant: Camilla Lloyd
Designed by: Tall Tree Ltd
Cover Make-up: Wladek Szechter

Previously published in four volumes for Dragon's World *Caves to Cathedrals, Science & Power, Scrolls to Computers* and *Wheels to Rockets.*

Printed in China

10 9 8 7 6 5 4 3 2 1

CONTENTS

Introduction

People have always wanted to travel in new ways, to conquer new parts of their environment. Three of the most fascinating fields of exploration have been the sea, the sky and space. Each has produced inventions that have transformed our world and expanded our knowledge.

For early people, the great fascination was the sea. They wanted to explore, to sail into the unknown and to use the water for transport in an age before there were wheels or even roads. It all began with the simplest of craft – log rafts and canoes made by hollowing out logs. But by the time of the ancient Egyptians, boats had become very sophisticated, with pointed hulls, sails and oars for steering. Boat-builders carried on improving their craft for thousands of years, producing vessels like the sleek ships of the Vikings and the super-fast clippers of the nineteenth century; boats that truly changed the world.

With the seas and rivers conquered, explorers and inventors looked to the skies. At first, they thought that they would need to build craft that copied birds' wings and many lost their lives testing these unworkable flying machines. But later engineers, such as the American brothers Wilbur and Orville Wright, had more success, improving their craft by trial and error until they produced machines that could fly safely. The Wrights' first aircraft, *Flyer*, was the ancestor of all other aeroplanes, from World War I fighters to modern airliners,

that enable us to achieve journeys in hours that once would have taken days or even weeks.

Beyond the sky was the 'final frontier', space. For many this was the greatest goal for exploration, but it seemed impossible to build a powerful enough vehicle to thrust its way out of the pull of the Earth's gravity. The answer was the rocket, invented long ago in ancient China, and developed for space travel by the Americans and Russians in the 1950s and 1960s. To begin with, the goal was to send human explorers into space, and the

Americans triumphed with the first visit to the Moon in 1969. But now most space exploration is unmanned, with space probes journeying long and far. Flying past the planets of our Solar System, such vehicles send back fascinating pictures and information. Now they are setting their sights still farther away, beyond the Solar System, as the endless search for new frontiers continues.

PHILIP WILKINSON

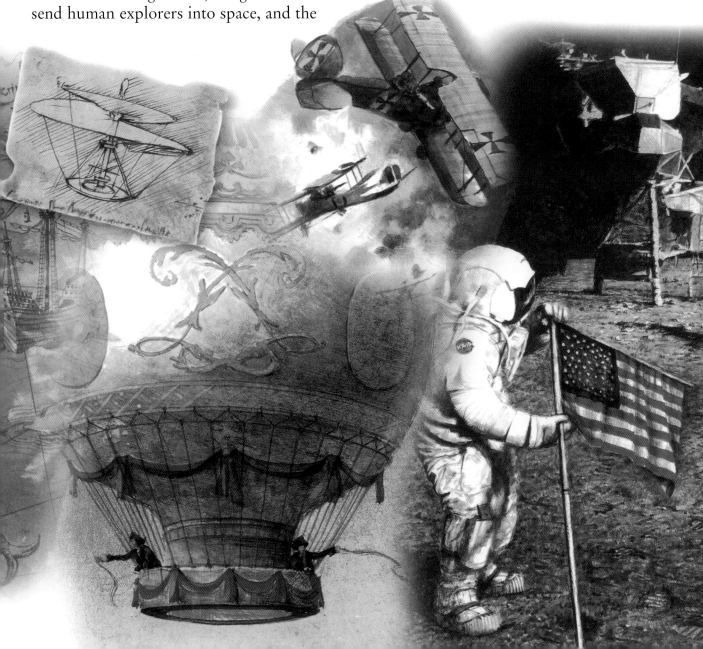

BOATS & SHIPS

From the earliest times, people realized that water could be used as a means of transport. Thousands of years of experiment and invention perfected the sailing ship as a vessel for trade and a weapon of war.

We have to go back into prehistory to imagine how people might have discovered that water was useful for transport. Early humans settled beside rivers and lakes where there was a water supply. The fish that could be caught from the banks were an added bonus.

FLOATING ON AIR

It was probably through observing floating logs and branches that people realized that they could use water to carry themselves and their goods. The first journeys by water may have been made by people holding on to tree trunks which had been washed downriver.

Then, someone discovered that objects containing air not only floated, but could also support a weight in the water. The next stage was to make floats of inflated animal skins sewn together tightly. Sealed clay pots were also used as floats. When skin or clay floats were bound together to make rafts, they could support a large platform carrying people or cargo.

△ *The earliest method of travel by water was probably to hold on to a floating log.*

△ *The first rafts were probably adapted from swimming floats, made of wood, skins or pots.*

△ *The coracle or quffa was one of the first craft to have high sides like a boat, rather than being flat.*

In shallow water, a raft could be driven along and steered with a pole long enough to reach to the river bed, but this was not possible where the water was deeper. The next development was to build a light raft with raised sides which could be pushed along with a paddle.

Early civilizations developed a wide variety of craft for transport or fishing. The dugout canoe was a tree-trunk with a hollow carved or burned into the middle. Archaeologists have found remains of dugouts dating from about 6300 BC.

However, dugouts could only be made in wooded places. In some places, a large basket-shaped frame was made from thin wood or wicker and animal skins were stretched tightly over it. These craft were built with simple tools such as flint knives and bone needles. They were so light that they could be picked up and

and pointed at each end to cut down the resistance of the water.

The Egyptians were also responsible for two further developments which were to change the history of travel by water. The first was the invention of the sail. Although it was easy to travel north down the Nile with the current, returning

Large ships were powered by rowing slaves who sat chained to benches.

carried on the back if necessary. Boats of this kind were used in Assyria before 6000 BC, and are still used in some places. In Britain, they are called 'coracles', and in the Middle East, 'quffas'.

REED BOATS

The civilization of ancient Egypt was the first to make a real effort to develop the technology of boat-building. The Egyptians lived along the River Nile, which could be sailed for about 1,200 kilometres, but there were no large trees in the area. The first Egyptian craft were rafts made out of the reeds that grew plentifully along the banks of the Nile. The reeds were tied in bundles and then bound tightly together. From simple rafts, the Egyptians went on to make reed boats, which were equipped with oars

home was hard work using just oars and paddles. At this time, the Egyptians grew cotton and were already skilled at weaving it into cloth. Observation of woven cotton hung out to dry must have given someone the idea of using wind power to propel boats. Sailors began to equip their boats with one large sail, made from tightly woven cotton and ropes to turn the sail into the wind. Oars could be used if the wind dropped.

THE RUDDER

The second important Egyptian innovation was the rudder. At first, this was simply a large paddle fixed at the boat's stern, with ropes to turn it. This made the steering independent of the oars and made movement in the water much more precise.

Reed boats were good for sailing up and down the river, but sturdier craft were needed at sea. The Egyptians began to build wooden boats from short planks of acacia, the only wood available. These boats were built up plank by plank, forming a hollow shell. With these boats, the Egyptians built up a large sea trade, exporting corn and cotton in return for jewels, spices, wood and metal.

FRAME-BUILT BOATS

Between 1500 and 1000 BC, a civilization grew up whose entire fortune was founded on seafaring trade. The Pheonicians lived at the eastern end of the

HOW SAILS WORK

The first sails were simply large rectangular sheets of cloth fixed to a mast at right-angles to the boat. In a following wind, that is one blowing in the direction of travel, these sails used the wind efficiently to carry the boat forward. But they did not work if the wind was blowing from any other direction.

Arab fishermen in the Red Sea and the Indian Ocean were probably the first sailors to use 'lateen' sails. The lateen is a triangular sail fixed to the mast along one side. The corner opposite the fixed side can be moved from side to side. This enables the sailor to adjust the position of the sail according to the direction of the wind. This is called 'trimming'. By trimming the sails, the boat can be 'tacked', or driven forward on a zig-zag course, even if it is sailing into the wind.

As sailing ships developed, they used combinations of square and lateen sails so that they could take advantage of all kinds of wind conditions. Each sail was controlled individually by ropes. Most ships had the square mainsails amidships to gather the wind and give the ship speed, while lateen sails at the bow and stern were trimmed to help the rudder control the ship's direction of travel.

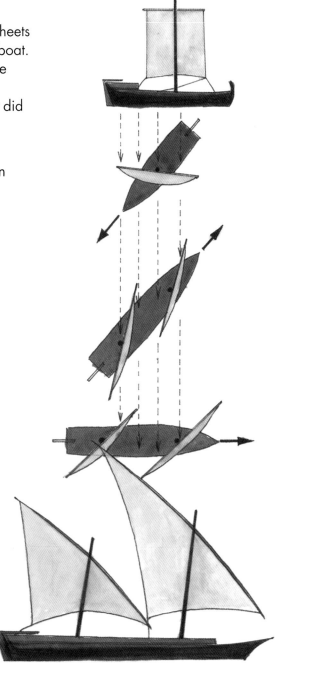

9

Mediterranean in what is now called Lebanon, and built the finest ships that had yet been seen. They were able to improve on Egyptian designs because they had tall cedar trees which they could use as keel and frame timbers. This meant that their ships were stronger and more suitable for long voyages at sea. For trading, they built 'round ships', which travelled slowly but could carry a large amount of cargo. Their most famous craft were the Phoenician longships, the first ships to be built for battle.

Longships had large, square sails. Wind power was backed up by men with oars, sometimes in two or three banks, one above the other. Built long and narrow, longships could cut through the water at a fast pace. At their bows, they had rams to attack enemy ships. With these

superior craft, the Phoenicians took command of the seas. From their home ports they explored the coasts of Africa, the Mediterranean and north-western Europe, setting up trading stations wherever they went.

CASTLES ON BOARD

Phoenician warships were designed to move in quickly to attack the enemy's fleet. If they were themselves attacked, they had little defence. The Greeks and Romans copied and improved on the Phoenicians ships.

The Romans gave their ships extra speed by adding a second sail at the bow, and designed a more accurate rudder with two paddles. In front of the stern, they built a structure which housed marines who were armed and ready to fight. This 'castle' was to become a feature of many large sailing ships, providing protection for the crew. The front part of a ship where the crew lives is still called the 'forecastle' or 'fo'c'sle'.

The Greeks and Romans changed the style of warfare at sea. Their warships, called 'galleys', were designed to carry troops for battle on the water. The galley would attack an enemy ship, and marines would fight on the decks of both. This kind of sea warfare was to continue for hundreds of years in Europe.

LATEEN SAILS

The Romans copied the square sails of the Phoenicians, but they also used triangular or lateen sails. The word lateen comes from 'Latin', the language of the Romans, but the triangular sail was developed many years before the days of the Roman Empire. It was first used by Arab sailors in the Red Sea and Indian Ocean. They sailed light, slim boats called 'dhows', with a triangular sail which ran

SAILING SHIPS

The fastest sailing ships ever built were called 'clippers'. They were ocean-going ships designed to carry perishable cargoes such as fruit and grain. The first clipper, the *Ann McKim*, was built in Baltimore, Maryland, USA, in 1832. There was keen competition for speed between clipper owners. One ship, the *Cutty Sark*, once covered 584 kilometres in one day's sailing. It took only 69 days to sail from Australia to Britain, compared with the normal one hundred days.

The largest sailing ship ever built was the *Great Republic*, launched in the United States in 1853 and intended to sail between the USA and Australia. While being prepared for its maiden voyage, it caught fire and sank, but it was later refloated and used as a troop-carrier in the American Civil War.

lengthways down the ship rather than across it. This enabled it to be trimmed, or turned, to take greater advantage of the wind. Roman galleys combined both kinds of sail, which made them more manoeuvrable in all kinds of weather.

VIKING RAIDERS

About 1,200 years ago, a new kind of ship was developed in northern Europe. The Vikings lived in Denmark, Norway and Sweden, where there was a good supply of timber. Their boats were the first to be 'clinker-built' – where each long plank of wood overlapped the one below.

△ *Egyptian shipwrights built ships from bundles of reeds or from short planks of wood joined together. The wooden boats looked like reed boats, with their high, curved ends.*

Viking longships, powered by a large, square sail and up to 80 oarsmen, carried out raids round the coasts of Europe and as far away as Greenland and North America. There was no protection for the crew, but longships were curved upwards at the bow and stern to help prevent them taking on too much water in high seas. The bow of the ship was often decorated with a figurehead of a

carved mythical figure such as a dragon. Viking ships were not intended for fighting at sea. The Vikings had the best ships, were the most fearless sailors of their time and were unlikely to meet any rivals on their voyages.

THE GALLEON

After the Vikings, the sail increasingly took over from oars as the major source of power for large ships, although oars were still carried for when there was no wind. By the fifteenth century, the three- or four-masted galleon, standing high out of the water, was being used for both trade and war. This was the kind of ship that took part in the great European voyages of exploration in the sixteenth and seventeenth centuries. In this period, too, European nations such as Spain, Portugal, France and Britain built up their navies with the aim of ruling the world's oceans. Heavy guns were introduced on ships about 1400, and, by the eighteenth century, a galleon could have as many as 100 heavy cannons aboard.

Around the world a great
variety of craft have developed
from the earliest rafts.
1 Masted outrigger canoes,
  South Pacific
2 Single masted reed boat,
  Lake Titicaca, South America
3 Modern windsurfer
4 Log raft
5 Junk, South China
6 Arabian dhow
7 Ancient Egyptian reed boat
8 Small sailing boat, South China
9 Wooden rowing boat, Europe
  and North America

By this time, there were a wide variety of ships at sea. The great battleships were backed up by smaller naval craft designed for speed and surprise attacks. Merchant ships ranged from large ocean-going galleons to small ships plying their trade along the coasts. Meanwhile, larger fishing-boats were built to range farther and farther from their home ports.

THE COMING OF STEAM

Towards the end of the eighteenth century, there was a development which was to signal the end of the days of sailing ships. In the 1780s, the first steamboats were built in America, driven by large oars powered by a steam engine. The boats were not a success, but other inventors took up the idea of using steam power for ships, and the next 100 years was a story of the triumph of steam and the gradual fading away of sail.

FINDING THE WAY

The first sailors had nothing to guide them except the Sun by day and the stars at night. The compass was the first of a number of aids to navigation that made travel by sea safer and easier.

Sailors, aircrews, motorists and even walkers use charts or maps to help them find the way to where they want to go. There are only a very few parts of the world, on land or sea, which have not been charted or mapped today.

Thousands of years ago, however, travellers had no maps to help them. If they were sailing in sight of land, or walking in an area they knew, they could rely on landmarks such as high cliffs or mountains to guide them. However, on the ocean, or in the middle of a desert or forest, there are no landmarks. Travellers had to find some other means of navigation.

FOLLOWING THE SUN

Early travellers kept their eyes on the sky. They knew that the Sun rose in one direction, climbed to a high point and then gradually sank until it set on the opposite side of the sky. Observing the Sun's position in the sky gave them some

△ *For thousands of years, a ship in the middle of the ocean could not tell exactly where it was.*

idea of the direction they were going.

At night, travellers could use the stars. North of the equator, they looked for the North Star, directly over the North Pole, as a pointer. In the southern hemisphere, they used the group of four stars called the Southern Cross, which points the way south. Navigating by the Sun or the stars was, of course, possible only when the sky was clear. Many travellers must have got lost when the sky clouded over.

Travelling became much easier when it was found that a small piece of lodestone, a brownish rock made of iron oxide, would always take up the same position in a line from north to south when allowed to swing freely. Lodestone is magnetic. It reacts to the Earth's magnetic field so that the north-seeking pole of the stone is attracted to the Earth's magnetic North Pole.

Someone must have observed that every time a small piece of lodestone was allowed to move freely,

▷ *Early maps were vague about the shape of coastlines and the precise location of islands or even continents.*

it took up a position in line with the Sun at midday and the North Star at night. Whoever first made this discovery was the inventor of the compass.

THE CHINESE COMPASS

About 400 BC, a Chinese writer described how overland travellers used a 'south-pointer' to help them find their way. Early Chinese compasses had a spoon-shaped piece of lodestone which was free to pivot on a polished bronze plate. The handle of the spoon pointed south.

The Chinese did not only use the compass for finding their way. There was an ancient Chinese belief that the exact siting of a building, including the direction it faced, was important for the happiness and good fortune of the people who lived in it. Before a house was built, an expert called a 'geomancer' was called in to advise on how it should be positioned, and he used a compass to come to his decision.

WHO INVENTED THE COMPASS?

Although the first written mention of the compass was in a Chinese book, the Chinese may not have been the first people to use the instrument. Some historians believe that the ancient Egyptians, or the Olmecs of ancient Mexico, made the discovery first, perhaps as long ago as 1000 BC.

What is certain is that by early in the twelfth century AD, Chinese sailors were using the compass at sea. By this time it had been discovered that an iron needle could be magnetized by rubbing it on a piece of lodestone. The needle could then be used as a pointer by floating it on a piece of cork or wood in a bowl of water.

THE NEEDLE COMPASS

Soon after this, the compass made its first appearance in Europe. How the knowledge travelled from east to west is not certain. Perhaps it came by way of the Islamic world, through Arab sailors, but this seems unlikely since the first Islamic descriptions of the compass are slightly later than those in Europe.

An early Chinese mariner's compass.

The first European to describe the compass was the English writer Alexander Neckham (1157–1217), in a book produced in 1187. At this time the compass needle was still being floated in water. In a book about magnetism published in 1269, the compass had taken on a more modern appearance. The needle was pivoted at the centre so that it could move freely, and was placed in a box with a glass cover. This made it a far more practical instrument for use at sea.

The most important innovation was a card at the bottom of the box which showed a circle divided into 360 degrees. This meant that the use of the compass by sailors had progressed well beyond the simple purpose of finding north and south. Using the 360 degree divisions, sailors could now plot a course and make corrections when they strayed from it.

DEAD RECKONING

There was still no way that sailors could work out their exact position. The best they could do with a compass was to find out in which direction they were moving. With the help of a system called 'dead reckoning', they could work out roughly how far they had travelled along their chosen course. For this, they needed an hour-glass and a long piece of rope with a log tied at the end.

▷ *It took centuries for the lodestone compass (top left) to develop into the compass we recognize today (top right). Once developed, accurate sea charts could be drawn with lines to show the compass bearings to various ports.*

THE SEARCH FOR AUSTRALIA

The invention of the sextant and the chronometer in the eighteenth century provided a new spur to exploration by European sailors. One of the most famous was Captain James Cook (1728–79).

Very little was known then about Australia, New Zealand, New Guinea and the smaller islands of the southern Pacific Ocean. The position of some islands, and parts of the coast of Australia, had been roughly mapped, and many people believed they were parts of a great southern continent, 'Terra Australis', that spread round the South Pole. Captain Cook's orders for his first expedition were to find out whether the southern Pacific was merely an ocean, or contained another great continent.

Cook set out in April 1769 and was away for 14 months. On his return, he was able to report that no 'great southern continent' existed. He had mapped and surveyed much of the coast of Australia, and had shown that there was open sea to the south between Australia and Antarctica.

The hour-glass was big enough to mark the passing of an hour or half an hour as the sand trickled from the top half into the bottom through a narrow neck. A junior member of the ship's crew was given the job of turning the hour-glass. At the same time, the rope, with knots tied at regular intervals, was paid out at the stern of the ship. A sailor counted each knot as it passed through his hands. When the top half of the hour-glass was empty, the number of knots since it had been turned over enabled the navigator to work out the speed of the ship. The speed of ships at sea is still measured in 'knots' today. A knot is one nautical mile (1,853 metres) per hour.

SUN AND STARS

If the sky was clear, sailors had another instrument which they could use to check their position. This was the 'astrolabe', invented in Greece about 200 BC. The astrolabe was a dial with a pointer that moved to measure the altitude of the Sun or the stars in degrees. This helped sailors to calculate the time and the ship's latitude, or position north or south of the equator. There was still no way of calculating a ship's longitude, or its position east or west.

The great European voyages of discovery, such as those of Ferdinand Magellan (c. 1480–1521) and Christopher Columbus (1451–1506), were made with only the astrolabe, the compass, the hour-glass and the log and line. However, these were the success stories. The dead reckoning method of calculating a position was very unreliable. Variations in winds and tides, or a moment's loss of concentration by the boy with the hour-glass or the sailor with the log and line, could throw the calculations badly wrong. For every successful voyage, there were many disasters when ships ran aground or simply got lost in the vast, empty oceans.

LOCAL TIME

In 1731, an English scientist, John Hadley (1682–1744), invented the sextant. This was an instrument for measuring the altitude of the Sun or stars, and was a great improvement on earlier methods such as the astrolabe. It provided an accurate measurement of the ship's latitude and of the 'local time' on board ship, but it still did not help with its position east or west.

ACCURATE TIME-KEEPING

What was needed was a means of showing the time at a known position so that it could be compared with the ship's local time. The difference between the two times would show the ship's distance east or west of the line of longitude passing through the known position. British ships, and eventually all the world's shipping, took the 'known position' to be Greenwich in south-east London.

The loss of ships at sea because of inaccurate navigation had become so serious by 1714 that the British Admiralty offered a prize of £20,000 to the maker of a chronometer accurate enough to keep time to within three seconds a day over a period of six weeks, even on a rough ocean voyage.

It was nearly fifty years before a clockmaker came up with the winning design. He was John Harrison (1693–1776), from Yorkshire in England. When his chronometer was tested on a voyage from London to the West Indies in 1761, it beat the Admiralty's requirements by losing only 2.7 seconds a day. For the first time, it was possible for sailors to work out their longitude as well as their latitude.

A SAFER MEANS OF TRAVEL

Although expensive at first, by about 1800, the chronometer was in general use among the western world's navies and merchant fleets.

△ *John Harrison's chronometer*

The chronometer brought about a revolution in ocean travel. As well as directly aiding navigation, the chronometer meant that coastlines and hidden rocks could be pinpointed more accurately on maps and charts. Shipping losses fell sharply, and business people were more ready to invest in carrying goods at sea. It was from this time that great shipping and trading companies began to make fortunes for those who invested in them, and the sea became a safer place for people who worked or travelled on it.

FLIGHT

For centuries, scientists, engineers and amateurs tried to fly with all kinds of strange machines. But it was two bicycle dealers from a small town in the United States who succeeded in making the first powered flight.

To be able to fly is one of the oldest human ambitions. In the ancient world, people looked at the birds in the sky and envied them. They told stories about imaginary winged gods and goddesses, and about bird-men such as Icarus whose father made him a pair of wings out of wax and feathers. Icarus flew too near the sun, which melted the wax and sent him plunging to his death. In real life, several people tried to imitate Icarus with wings made of various materials, but all with disastrous results.

COPYING THE BIRDS

It was natural that people should think that the way to fly would be to design a machine with flapping wings like a bird's. The famous artist Leonardo da Vinci (1452–1519) made drawings of just such a machine, with wings that were flapped by the pilot's arms, but he never built it.

As it turned out, the first humans to take to the air did so in a very different way. In 1783, two French brothers,

△ *In myth, Icarus flew by attaching bird's feathers to his arms with wax. Early inventors often tried to copy the birds.*

The first human flight was made by the Montgolfiers' balloon in 1783. It was not until the middle of the nineteenth century that powered and steerable airships were produced.

Joseph-Michel (1740–1810) and Jacques-Etienne (1745–99) Montgolfier, built and successfully flew a hot-air balloon.

But balloons were at the mercy of the wind for their direction and speed, so they were no use as a means of transport. Attempts to build a true flying machine continued. A number of nineteenth-century experimenters had some success with gliders. An Englishman, Sir George Cayley (1773–1857), designed the first successful passenger-carrying glider in 1853. Cayley worked out the principle of 'lift' which is obtained by making the upper surface of the wing convex, thereby keeping the wing airborne.

The greatest glider pioneer of the age was a German, Otto Lilienthal (1848–96). He made about 2,000 flights in craft he had built himself, but in 1896, a glider that he was flying spun out of control and crashed, killing him. He was only one of many pioneer aviators whose experiments ended in fatal accidents.

FLYING BY STEAM

Other inventors tried making steam-powered aircraft. One of these was Clement Ader (1841–1926), a French engineer. In 1890, he claimed his craft had flown for about 50 metres, but this success was never repeated. Meanwhile, a number of American inventors had become interested in flying. One, Samuel Langley (1834–1906), built both steam-powered and petrol-engined aircraft, but neither carried a pilot. The achievement of building the first powered aircraft to make a manned flight went to two American brothers, Orville (1871–1948) and Wilbur (1867–1912) Wright, from Dayton, Ohio.

The Wright brothers ran a bicycle business, but in their spare time they gave all their attention to aeronautics. They had no engineering training, but they studied the scientific principles of flight, read all they could about the pioneer flights of the Europeans and carried out countless experiments with model kites and gliders. They even built their own wind tunnel in their workshop to test the performance of different shapes of wings and propellers.

GETTING IT RIGHT

The Wrights saw that there were three problems to be overcome before powered flight was possible. The first was to make wings large enough to take the weight of the engine and passenger, and to keep the

THE DREAM OF FLIGHT

Before serious experimentation began, many people had wondered about the possibilities of human flight. Many of their ideas look bizarre today, but at the time the experience of flight they had was from watching birds.

Many ancient stories involve people flying relying on magic devices or the power of birds (top left). The first designs for flying machines were often just as impossible, like the airship design (above) which was supposed to be lifted by vacuums in the four spheres. Even the great thinker Leonardo da Vinci failed in his ornithopter design because he forgot to take account of the weight of the wood.

In the nineteenth century, however, inventors such as George Cayley and Otto Lilienthal began to make the dream of flight a possibility.

Leonardo's ornithopter

Leonardo da Vinci

Georgy Cayley

Otto Lilienthal

Lilienthal's glider

Cayley's flying top

Cayley's glider

aircraft in the air. The second was to find the right engine. The third, and perhaps most important, was to work out ways of balancing and steering the aircraft in flight. It was the problem of controlling aircraft in flight that had defeated previous attempts.

The solution that the Wrights worked out to the last problem was to provide their aircraft with controllable surfaces similar to those found on aircraft today. They fitted a movable elevator in front of the wings, and a movable tail fin which acted as a rudder. After experimenting on gliders, in the autumn of 1902, the Wrights set out to build a powered flying machine.

Wilbur and Orville Wright

FAILURE AT KITTY HAWK

The Wrights worked carefully, meticulously testing and double-checking each part of their machine as they went along. At last, in December 1903, everything was ready for the great moment. The brothers had chosen for their first flight an area of sand hills called Kill Devil Hills near Kitty Hawk in North Carolina.

Flyer, as the Wrights named their aircraft, was a biplane with a wing-span of 12 metres. It was powered by a four-cylinder petrol engine mounted in the middle of the lower wing. The engine drove two wooden propellers fitted behind the wings so that they pushed the aircraft through the air. The pilot lay on his front across the lower wing beside the engine, with a bar in front to hold on to. *Flyer* had no wheeled undercarriage. It would take off from a set of wheels mounted on a rail track, and land on

skids shaped like skis. Including the pilot, *Flyer* weighed 340 kilograms.

On 14 December, *Flyer* was placed in position ready for take-off. Orville and Wilbur tossed a coin to decide who should make the first flight. Wilbur won, and took his position on the lower wing. The engine was started, and *Flyer*, with Wilbur aboard began to move along the take-off track.

Then disaster struck. Perhaps through nerves, Wilbur made a mistake in his setting of the elevator so that *Flyer* could not rise. It ran to the end of the rail, hit the sand barrier and came to a grinding halt, badly damaged. It must have seemed to the Wrights that all their years of hard work had ended in failure.

TAKE-OFF AT LAST

It was three days before repairs to *Flyer* were finished and the Wrights were ready to try again. This time, it was Orville's turn to be pilot. The engine was started and *Flyer* began to move. It lifted away from the ground, coming to the ground safely 42 metres away.

The first powered flight had lasted a mere 12 seconds, but it was a start. Later the same day, the brothers, taking turns as pilot, made three more flights. On the last of these, Wilbur made up for his mistake of three days before by staying in the air for 49 seconds and covering 260 metres at a top speed of 48 kilometres per hour.

After the fourth landing, the brothers left *Flyer* standing on the sand and took a much-needed break. While they were standing talking, the wind got up, and a

The Wright brothers tested and re-tested everything before they attempted powered flight. Soon they were taking longer and longer flights, learning to control the aircraft in the air.

DOGFIGHTS

Early in World War I, aircraft were used for the first time to observe and report on enemy movements at the battlefront. These were small single- or two-seater fighters armed with machine-guns. Later in the war, heavier aircraft carried out bombing missions over enemy territory.

There was bitter rivalry between the fighter pilots of the warring countries. The 'dogfights' between them provided an exciting show for people on the ground, but the fights often ended in the death of one or both pilots.

The most famous of the World War I fighter pilots was a German, Baron Manfred von Richtofen (1892–1918). He was nicknamed 'the Red Baron'. He claimed to have shot down 80 British and French aircraft in dogfights. He died just before the war ended, shot down behind British lines.

sudden gust caught the plane. The wings lifted, and the light aircraft rolled helplessly over and over. When it stopped, its wings were damaged, some of their supports were smashed and the engine had broken adrift. On its day of glory, the Wrights' first aircraft had made its last landing. For the brothers, it was back to the drawing board to start designing *Flyer II*.

CRASHING SILENCE

You might think that the Wrights' four successful flights would have made headline news all over the world the following morning. Amazingly, however, the story didn't even make the pages of the local morning paper in the Wrights' home town. People who went in for flying were often written off as cranks attempting the impossible. Even if it were possible, others said, it would be done by trained engineers, not by a couple of small-town enthusiasts. So the Wrights' achievement went almost unnoticed at the time. This did not worry them much. They were convinced, whatever anyone else thought, that powered flight had a future. The brothers returned to their workshop and started planning the improvements they were going to make in *Flyer II*.

The Wright brothers knew that there was a long way to go before flying would be completely safe and reliable. With *Flyer II* and *Flyer III*, they gradually increased the length of their flights and the manoeuvrability of their aircraft in the air. In October 1905, *Flyer III* flew for a total of 38 minutes, covering 38 kilometres. The flight included demonstrations of banking, turning, circling and flying a long course in a figure-of-eight.

SELLING THE IDEA

By now, the Wright brothers were convinced that aircraft had a useful future and planned to go into business making them. But who would buy one? They tried the United States Army, suggesting that aircraft could watch enemy positions from the air and carry messages. At first, the Army was not interested, so in 1908 Wilbur set off for Europe by ship with a demonstration machine to try to sell aircraft there.

Europe welcomed flying with enthusiasm. The kings of the United Kingdom, Italy and Spain came to see Wilbur Wright's demonstration. More importantly for the future of flying, so did Lord Northcliffe (1865–1922), the owner of a British newspaper, the *Daily*

Mail. The *Mail* splashed the news of a prize for the first person to fly across the English Channel from France to England. This spurred on both amateur and professional engineers to have a go at making their own machines. The prize was won in 1909 by a Frenchman, Louis Blériot (1872–1936). By this time, everyone was talking about flying. At last, people began to see what it could mean. The Wrights had all the publicity they needed – the air age had arrived.

AIRCRAFT AT WAR

It was not long before the reason for Europe's keen interest in aircraft became clear. Rivalry between Britain and Germany for industrial power, and the old enmity between Germany and France, were leading steadily towards war. When war came in 1914, aircraft were to play a small but important part in it. By now, aircraft could reach speeds approaching 161 kilometres per hour. Germany, France, Britain and Italy all

▷ *After World War I, flying circuses became a popular attraction. People would gather to see the flimsy flying machines loop-the-loop and fly upside down. Some people had their first taste of flying at these events, paying to go up for short flights.*

produced small fighter aircraft like the British Sopwith Camel for use at the fighting front, and heavier bombers to make raids deep into enemy territory. The need for better weapons was a spur to improvements. Most governments added a third fighting service, an air force, to the old forces of the army and navy.

FLYING FOR PEACE

In 1919, the airfields of Europe and America were full of aircraft, and there were thousands of trained pilots and navigators. However, could flying be adapted for peaceful uses?

Charles Lindbergh

The years after World War I were a time when aviators competed with each other to score 'firsts'. In 1919, two British flyers, John Alcock (1892–1919) and Arthur Whitten Brown (1886–1948), made the first flight across the Atlantic.

In 1927, an American, Charles Lindbergh (1902–74), made the first solo trans-atlantic flight from New York to Paris. Five years later a Scottish pilot, James Mollison (1905–59) made the first

trans-atlantic solo flight from east to west. The first flight across the Pacific was in 1928 by two Australians, Charles Kingsford Smith (1897–1935) and Charles Ulm (1898–1934).

Women also took part in these pioneer flights. Amy Johnson (1903–41), an Englishwoman, flew solo from Britain to Australia in 1930, and followed this up with many other record-breaking flights. The American aviator, Amelia Earhart (1898–1937), became the first woman to fly the Atlantic in 1932. Five years later, Earhart disappeared in an attempt to fly around the world from California.

POST IN THE AIR

By this time, flying was not just a few enthusiasts making record-breaking flights. Governments and business people alike had begun to recognize it as a useful and profitable means of transport.

The postal services were among the leaders in taking advantage of the speed of flying. The very first airmail service began as early as 1911 in Britain. Letters and postcards were carried between London and Windsor as part of the celebrations for the coronation of King George V, but the service operated for only a few weeks.

In 1919, the British Post Office started a regular air mail service between London and Paris. This was later extended to other European cities and by 1921 to the Middle East. Meanwhile, in 1920, the United States Post Office began flying mail between San Francisco and New York, with a number of stops on the way.

THE FIRST AIRLINES

By the 1920s, most people were used to seeing aircraft in the air, and flying no longer seemed to be defying nature. Flying was still considered a sport or a novelty, and many people had their first experience of flying when they went up for 'joy rides' lasting for a few minutes. However, would they travel by air?

A number of airlines were founded in the 1920s, particularly in countries like Britain, France and the Netherlands which had large empires scattered across the world. The first passenger planes were tiny, some carrying only eight passengers. Some early airlines flew wartime bombers which had been fitted with seats, and some seated their passengers in loose wicker armchairs. But soon the aircraft industry began to build planes specially designed for comfortable passenger travel.

THE DAKOTA

In the USA, where there were huge overland distances to be covered, air travel really took off. American aircraft builders moved into the lead, and 1936 saw the first flight of a plane that was to

ALCOCK AND BROWN

John Alcock and Arthur Whitten Brown made the first nonstop flight across the Atlantic in 1919. Twenty-seven-year-old Alcock was a test pilot for the Vickers Aircraft Company. He chose a World War I Vickers Vimy two-engined bomber, fitted with extra petrol tanks, for the flight. Brown, who was 33, went with him as a navigator.

On 14 June 1919, the two men set out from St John's, Newfoundland in Canada. Sixteen hours and 12 minutes later they landed at Clifden, County Galway in Ireland.

Alcock and Brown shared a prize of £10,000 given by the British newspaper the *Daily Mail*. Both were also given knighthoods. But for Alcock, the triumph was short-lived. Six months later, he crashed and was killed while flying from England to France.

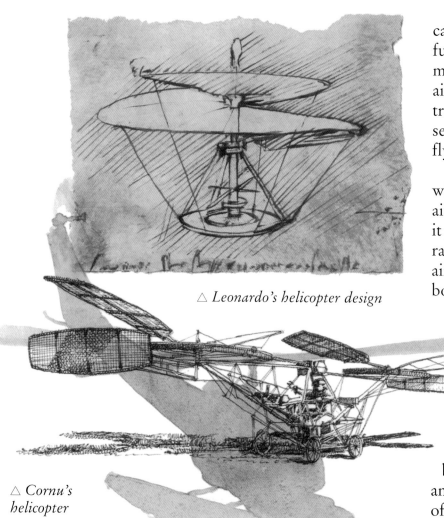

△ *Leonardo's helicopter design*

△ *Cornu's helicopter*

carry larger amounts of fuel. They soon took over many of the world's longer air routes. The first trans-atlantic passenger services were operated by flying boat in 1938.

It was only after 1945, when improvements in aircraft technology made it possible to build long-range conventional aircraft, that the flying boat went out of favour.

THE HELICOPTER

Meanwhile, an entirely different kind of aircraft, the helicopter, had appeared. Helicopters use spinning rotor blades to move forward and also to hover. The idea of giving an aircraft lift by spinning some kind of device above it was an old one. In the early sixteenth century, Leonardo da Vinci drew a sketch of a machine like this, with a platform suspended from large spinning blades.

Sir George Cayley, the British inventor who had experimented with gliders, began to work on the idea of the helicopter some 300 years after Leonardo. In 1843, he produced a steam-powered design, but it was never built. A real helicopter had to await the invention of the internal combustion engine.

GROUND TEST

The attraction of an aircraft which could take off and land vertically, avoiding the need for runways, continued to appeal to engineers, and in 1917 the first working

dominate air travel for many years. This was the Douglas DC3, also called the Dakota. It carried 21 passengers and flew at about 270 kilometres per hour. The DC3 became the most widely used plane among the world's airlines, carrying mail, passengers and cargo over short distances. By 1944, over 10,000 were flying. Some are still in use today.

FLYING BOATS

Problems began to emerge as more heavily laden airliners took to the skies. They needed increasingly long runways and also had to make frequent stopovers to take on more fuel. In the 1930s, a new kind of airliner appeared. Flying boats took off and landed on water, and could helicopter was made by Louis-Charles Breguet (1880–1955). Four large rotors, or sets of circulating blades, were arranged around the pilot, who sat in the centre of the machine. The helicopter never actually took off. It was tested while being tethered to the ground, but it achieved a lift of 1.5 metres.

In the same year, another Frenchman, Paul Cornu (1881–1944), made a helicopter which actually made a few brief, low flights. But he had to abandon his experiments because of lack of money.

THE AUTOGIRO

The next important step came in 1923 in Spain, when Juan de la Cierva (1895–1936) demonstrated an aircraft which he called an 'autogiro'. This had a four-bladed rotor above the fuselage, but each blade was hinged so that it could move up and down during flight. Unlike a

helicopter, the autogiro's rotor blades were not driven by the engine. They went round as the aircraft was driven forward by its propeller. In fact, the autogiro was part helicopter and part aeroplane. It could not take off or land absolutely vertically, but it did so at a steep angle, avoiding the need for a large airfield. Unlike a helicopter, it could not hover.

Many enthusiasts thought the autogiro might develop into an aerial form of personal transport. Nothing came of these hopes, because the autogiro was overtaken by the helicopter, which could take off and land vertically.

The inventor of the first successful helicopter was Igor Sikorsky (1889–1972). He had experimented with helicopters in Russia, his home country, since 1909, but then turned his interest to fixed-wing aircraft. In the 1930s, he came back to helicopters, and in 1939, his first successful machine, the VS-300, made its maiden flight. Since then, the helicopter has found many uses, like personal transport, troop-carrying, for search and rescue work and in industry.

▽ *The hovering ability of the helicopter makes it a vital tool for rescue services. It can hover over a spot that is inaccessible otherwise, so that rescue workers can be lowered in and injured people can be carried away.*

THE JET ENGINE

On the eve of World War II, unknown to each other, a German and a British inventor raced against time to produce a jet-engined aircraft. Their work resulted in the fast, comfortable intercontinental air travel we enjoy today.

Although jet aircraft were not flown regularly until the 1940s, the idea of an engine producing power by shooting out a stream of gases and compressed air behind it goes back a long way. It is said that the British scientist Sir Isaac Newton (1642–1727) thought of using the idea in a steam carriage as long ago as 1687. Two hundred years later an aeroplane driven by steam jets was designed, although it was never built.

Then, at the beginning of the twentieth century, the gas turbine was invented.

This works by using hot exhaust gases to drive a turbine, in a similar way to a jet engine. Gas turbines were used in industry, and some people began to wonder if they could be adapted to power aircraft.

THE FIRST JET ENGINE
One such person was a British Royal Air Force officer, Frank Whittle (1907–96). Whittle began researching the idea of a gas turbine aircraft engine while he was still a student. By the time he was

△ Concorde *was taken out of service in 2003.*

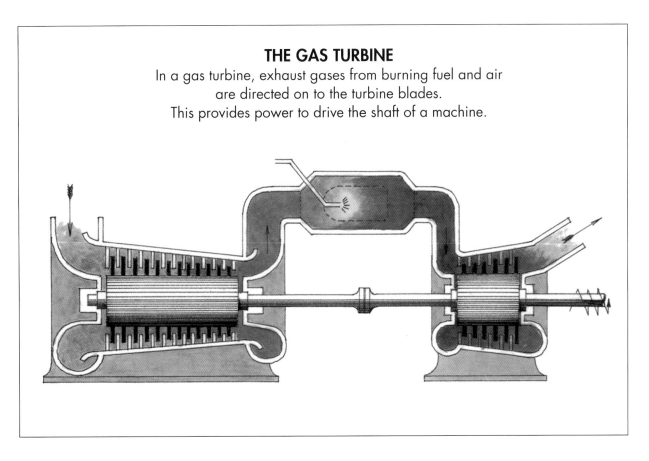

THE GAS TURBINE
In a gas turbine, exhaust gases from burning fuel and air
are directed on to the turbine blades.
This provides power to drive the shaft of a machine.

23, he had designed a jet engine for use in aircraft, although he lacked the money to build one himself. His RAF employers allowed him time off to work on the project, but showed little interest in the results.

Finally, in 1937, Whittle found some backers to finance the building of his jet engine. This was given its first test runs in the same year. There were teething troubles, but Whittle and his team carried on. Then, in 1938, with war looming, the RAF began to take an interest in Whittle's work and gave him the support he needed to speed it up. Two years later, the engine was ready to go into production, and Britain's top engineering firm, Rolls-Royce, was chosen to make it.

Sir Frank Whittle

RACE WITH THE GERMANS
Meanwhile, unknown to Whittle, a German aeronautical engineer was working on similar lines. His name was Hans Pabst von Ohain (1911–98).

Unlike Whittle, von Ohain did not have to struggle to find backers. One of Germany's leading manufacturers of aircraft, Heinkel, gave him a job and all the research support he needed. Von Ohain was later than Whittle in producing the first engine, but he was the first to get a jet-engined aircraft into the air, on 27 August 1939, just one week before World War II broke out. It was May 1941 before the first British jet aircraft, the Gloster Whittle E28, was ready to fly.

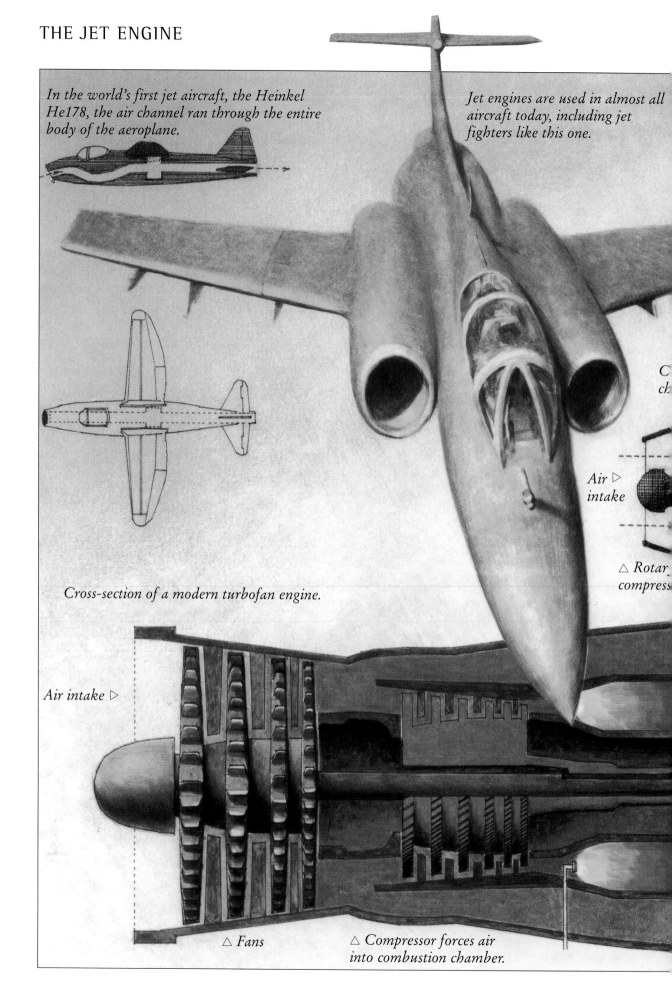

In the world's first jet aircraft, the Heinkel He178, the air channel ran through the entire body of the aeroplane.

Jet engines are used in almost all aircraft today, including jet fighters like this one.

C
ch

Air ▷
intake

△ Rotar
compress

Cross-section of a modern turbofan engine.

Air intake ▷

△ Fans

△ Compressor forces air into combustion chamber.

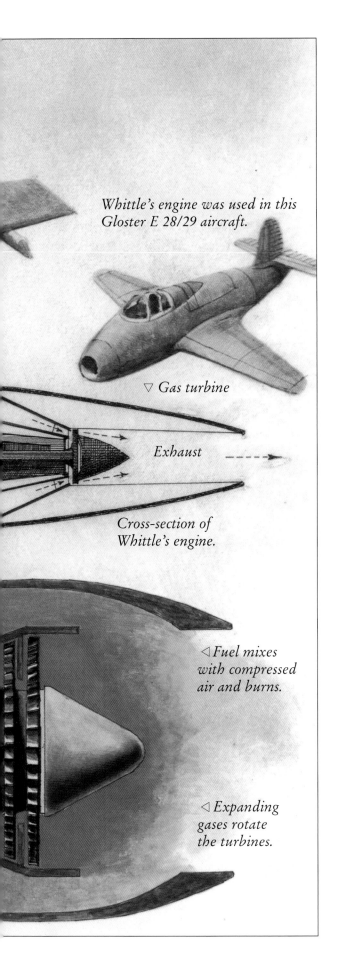

Whittle's engine was used in this Gloster E 28/29 aircraft.

▽ Gas turbine

Exhaust

Cross-section of Whittle's engine.

◁ Fuel mixes with compressed air and burns.

◁ Expanding gases rotate the turbines.

JETS AT WAR

Events move quickly in wartime, and both the British and German air forces hurried to build jet aircraft. Their first jet fighters went into service in 1944, just as World War II was reaching its crucial final stages. The increased speed of jet aircraft enabled them to move swiftly into action, surprising the crews of slower piston-engined planes.

The first aircraft to go into production using Whittle's jet engine was the twin-engined Gloster Meteor which could reach a speed of 625 kilometres per hour. The first German jet fighter was the Messerschmidt 262, also twin-engined. The 262 could out-fly the Meteor with a maximum speed of 869 kilometres per hour, but because it had been rushed into service too soon, it had some troublesome design faults.

In spite of a few teething problems, in the remaining years of World War II, both of these aircraft demonstrated that the jet engine provided air forces with a powerful new weapon.

Meanwhile, in the USA, a team of Whittle's engineers had been advising the United States Army Air Force on jet engines. The first American jet, the Lockheed *Shooting Star*, first flew in October 1942, but the war had ended before it went into service with the US Air Force. Soon, Russia had its first jet aircraft, the MiG 15, and other countries followed suit.

JET AIRLINERS

When peace came in 1945, the jet technology that had been developed for use in warplanes could be applied to civilian aircraft. One of the problems for airlines before the war had been the inefficiency of piston engines. This meant that they had to carry huge amounts of fuel, and even then had to make frequent stops to take on more. The greater efficiency of jets made the development of jet airliners attractive, especially for intercontinental flights. Not only could jets fly faster, they could also fly higher. This improved their efficiency even more, and also gave a smoother and more comfortable flight for passengers as jets could fly above the clouds, so avoiding any bad weather.

As the new jet airliners carrying larger numbers of passengers came into service, the cost of air travel fell. In the USA, even in the 1930s, it had become commonplace to make long journeys between the major cities by air. Now, all over the world, flying lost its pre-war luxury image and became the normal means of travel for people going abroad on holiday or business trips. A new generation of airliners, the huge jumbo jets, was built to cope with the vast numbers of people who now wanted to travel by air.

A whole family of jet engines had been developed from the simple original design. One of these was the turbofan. The front cover of the engine conceals a fan which sucks air in and passes it to a compressor before the air and fuel mixture is ignited. The turbofan operates more quietly and uses less fuel than other types of jet engine. Turbofans were used to power the new wide-bodied jumbos.

FASTER THAN SOUND

Once the jet engine had been developed, the race was on to build engines that would drive aircraft at ever greater speeds. The lead was taken by the world's major air forces. They wanted jet fighters that could fly faster than the enemy's, and jet bombers that could fly high and fast, out of reach of enemy defences.

'Breaking the sound barrier' became an important target. Sound travels in air at about 1,160 kilometres per hour. At one time, it was thought that at speed like this the pressure on aircraft frames, and

▽ Concorde *had a cruising speed of 2,300 kilometres per hour.*

JUMP-JETS

The thrust of gases from a jet engine pushes an aircraft forwards. Some engineers reasoned that if this thrust was pointed towards the ground, it would also give an aircraft enough lift to take off. This reasoning has led to the development of vertical takeoff and landing aircraft, or 'VTOLs', for military use. Warplanes are often required to take off from ships or in other confined spaces. VTOLs can operate from small aircraft carriers or from jungle clearings. They are among the fastest and most agile aircraft in the sky today.

on the bodies of their pilots, would be too much. This was disproved in 1947 when an American Bell X-1 aircraft, powered by a rocket engine, broke the sound barrier without mishap. There was no reason why suitably designed aircraft should not fly at supersonic speeds.

SUPERSONIC PASSENGER TRAVEL

Once this was known, the world's air forces began to equip themselves with supersonic bombers and fighter aircraft. Airlines, too, were attracted by the thought of supersonic flight. The costs of developing a supersonic airliner are huge, and so far only two have ever gone into service. One was the Russian Tupolev 144, and the other was *Concorde*, jointly developed by Britain and France.

Concorde provided flights across the Atlantic between 1976 and 2003.

Both planes were disappointments. The Tupolev 144 had technical problems and was withdrawn from regular use. *Concorde* never earned the money that was spent on it. This is partly because it carried only 128 passengers, making fares very expensive. There were other problems with *Concorde*. It was very noisy and had to be grounded for a long period after a fatal accident.

Although *Concorde* could cross the Atlantic twice as fast as a conventional jet, most people preferred to continue to travel slower but more cheaply. Scientists are still working on jet technology, to try to achieve supersonic speed at a lower cost and with less noise.

ROCKETS

When the ancient Chinese let off the first rockets, they could not have dreamed that these toys would one day lead to the exploration of space, landings on the Moon and worldwide communications.

Like a jet engine, a space rocket uses the backward rush of exhaust gases to propel itself forward. In a jet engine, the gases are produced by the burning of fuel mixed with the oxygen found in the Earth's atmosphere. However, a space rocket contains its own supply of oxygen as well as the fuel to be burned with it. This is why space rockets are able to continue to operate outside the Earth's atmosphere, for as long as their fuel lasts. The first rockets had nothing to do with travel at all, however.

THE FIRST ROCKETS

The ancient Chinese were probably the first people to use rockets made with gunpowder as fireworks. They probably also attached rockets to arrows. Although not very accurate, these missiles would certainly have frightened the enemy.

△ *In ancient China, rockets were used as fireworks or as weapons to terrify enemies.*

▷ *The unknown realms of space have been the subject of many books and films. Space travel was a fantasy when Jules Verne and H.G. Wells wrote about it, but today it is reality. How many other space fantasies will become facts in the future?*

△ *In the 1770s, Hyder Ali who usurped the crown of Mysore in India, built explosive rockets as weapons against the British army.*

the idea. By 1805, he had developed a rocket for use at sea as an attack weapon. It was first used in the following year, both at sea and on land. Congreve's rocket was so successful that a Rocket Brigade of the British army was formed to specialize in rocket warfare. But improvements in firearms and artillery made them more accurate and efficient than rockets, so the science of rocket warfare was abandoned for a time.

Knowledge of gunpowder passed from China to Europe by way of the Islamic world. About 1250, the English scientist Roger Bacon (c. 1214–92) wrote down the formula for gunpowder. About 100 years later a German monk, Berthold Schwarz (fourteenth century), invented the first firearms. Soon gunpowder was being produced all over Europe for use in guns, and inventors began to think about using it in rockets.

ROCKETS AT WAR

One of the most successful inventors was an eighteenth-century Indian prince, Hyder Ali (1728–82). He and his son Tippu Sultan (1749–99) built rockets with a metal container in which the fuel was burned. The metal containers could withstand greater explosions, giving the rockets more thrust. These Indian rockets were used in battles against the British in India in 1792 and again in 1799.

The British were impressed and began to investigate rockets for themselves. Sir William Congreve (1772–1828), a scientist employed by the British army, worked on

DREAMS THAT CAME TRUE

The idea of travelling into space with the help of rockets was first put forward by writers of science fiction. In 1865, the French writer Jules Verne (1828–1905) published a story called *From the Earth to the Moon*. The British author H.G. Wells (1866–1946) also wrote about adventures in space involving rocket propulsion. Although these stories were fiction, they were based on real scientific theories. It is surprising how close to the reality of space travel many of their ideas were.

▷ *Although Verne's and Wells' stories were works of the imagination, they were based on scientific theories of the time. The first space rockets reflected their stories and the first moves towards rocket-powered travel began only 50 years after Jules Verne published* From the Earth to the Moon.

1 *Tsiolkovski's space ship*
2 *Goddard's liquid-propelled rocket*
3 *German* V-2 *rocket*
4 *Inside a* V-2 *rocket*
5 *Multi-stage rocket showing its different stages*
6 *The* Saturn V *rocket, which took the manned* Apollo *craft to the Moon*

LIQUID FUEL

In Russia in 1895, Konstantin Tsiolkovski (1857–1935) began to write seriously about the possibilities of space travel. He had given some thought to the problem of making a rocket powerful enough to escape from the Earth's gravitational pull. Tsiolkovski's idea was to use a mixture of liquid hydrogen and oxygen as fuel.

At about the same time, in the United States, an American teenager called Robert Goddard (1882–1945) was thinking about the possibility of travelling to Mars. It was believed in the 1890s that the so-called 'canals' observed on Mars by astronomers were evidence that some form of human life existed there. So Mars became the focus of scientists' thoughts about space travel.

Robert Goddard became fascinated with thoughts of rocket-powered travel in space. He became a leading physicist and a professor at Clark University in Massachusetts. In 1914, he began designing rocket engines, and five years later published a forecast that rockets would one day carry a camera to the far side of the Moon.

Yuri Gagarin, the first man in space.

By 1926, Goddard was ready to test his first liquid-propelled rocket. In 1930, one of his rockets reached a height of 610 metres, travelling at 804 kilometres per hour. Five years later, he sent up a rocket which broke the sound barrier.

ROCKETS AT WAR

Robert Goddard's work was reported in scientific journals and aroused interest in Europe. Societies for rocket research and space exploration were formed. One of these was based in Berlin, Germany, and was founded by a young engineering student, Wernher von Braun (1912–77). His society obtained the use of a plot of land near Berlin as a rocket-launching site. By 1931, one of von Braun's rockets had reached a height of 1.609 kilometres.

At this time, the German government was forbidden to make weapons by the Peace Treaty after World War I. However, the Treaty said nothing about rockets, so the government funded von Braun's rocket research. He turned his attention from space travel to weaponry, and in 1936, he was put in charge of a secret rocket research station at Peenemünde. It was here that he developed the *V-2* guided missile, a terrifying weapon launched against Britain in the closing stages of World War II. By April 1945, 4,000 *V-2s* had been fired.

RIVALS FOR ROCKETRY

It was clear that Germany was the world leader in rocket technology and that rockets provided a means of delivering powerful weapons over long distances. The two rival superpowers, the USA and the then USSR, both wanted German rocket technology.

Wernher von Braun, who had surrendered to the American army in 1945, went with his team to the USA. Other German scientists went to the USSR. The division of knowledge about rockets led to the 'space race' of the 1960s and 1970s between the two superpowers. At the same time, both countries

SPACE LITTER

In the past 40 years, hundreds of satellites have been launched into orbit. Some were programmed to send back information for a limited period of time, and then stop. Others never functioned properly, and simply keep on going round uselessly.

There is no way of knowing how many pieces of this space junk are still in orbit around the Earth, or even further out in space beyond orbit. Some are diverted off course by collision with meteorites and veer towards the Earth, burning up as they reach the atmosphere. The rest, out of control because their communications systems are broken, may orbit the Earth for centuries.

There are also tools and pieces of equipment which have been lost or dumped by astronauts. Lunar vehicles have been abandoned on the Moon, and some of the planets now carry the remains of space probes which have been deliberately crashed into them. The people of Earth have explored space, but they have also polluted it.

▽ *Neil Armstrong, Buzz Aldrin and Michael Collins (1930–), who travelled to the Moon in Apollo 11.*

competed to develop rocketry as a method of delivering nuclear weapons.

RUSSIA SCORES A FIRST

Both the USA and the USSR worked on similar lines. The first essential in space exploration was to break free of the Earth's gravitational pull. Before that, however, there was the possibility of putting objects in orbit, held at a distance from the Earth by gravity but still free to circle the planet. In December 1957, the USSR's *Sputnik 1* became the first satellite to achieve this. Its distinctive

'bleep' as it circled the earth became a wonder of the world. The space race was now on in earnest, and America's rocket team, led by Wernher von Braun, redoubled its efforts.

America responded a few months after *Sputnik 1* with its own artificial satellite, *Explorer 1*, but by this time the USSR was even further ahead. Just one month after the launch of *Sputnik 1*, they had launched *Sputnik 2*, this time carrying a dog named Laika, the first live passenger in space!

Two years later, the USSR was the first to put a manned craft in space, when Yuri Gagarin (1934–68) orbited the Earth. The Americans followed a month later, sending astronaut Alan B. Shepard (1923–) into space for just fifteen minutes. Then, on 16 July 1969, the world heard that Jules Verne's fantasy of

◁ *As he stepped on to the surface of the Moon, Neil Armstrong spoke his famous words, 'That's one small step for man, one giant leap for mankind'.*

▽ *The first spacecraft could only be used once, but the space shuttle is designed to be reusable.*

100 years before had come true. US astronauts Neil Armstrong (1930–) and Edwin 'Buzz' Aldrin (1930–) had landed on the surface of the Moon.

A CHANGED WORLD

There have been many exciting space exploits since then, all made possible by rocket technology. However, rocket-launched satellites have changed our lives in many more everyday ways. Satellite television has made it possible for us to receive dozens of different programmes at home.

News from the other side of the world can be beamed to us by satellite while it is still happening. Satellites carry international telephone calls, keep a watch on the world's weather, provide aids to navigation for sailors and aircrews, report on the movements of troops of potential enemies and provide a wealth of valuable information for astronomers and other scientists. In just a few decades, rocket technology has changed our lives.

FIND OUT SOME MORE

After you have read about the ideas and inventions in this book, you may want to find out some more information about them. There are lots of books devoted to specific topics, such as ships or space travel, so that you can discover more facts. All over Britain and Ireland, you can see historical sites and visit museums that contain historical artefacts that will tell you more about the subjects that interest you. The books, sites and museums listed below cover some of the most important topics in this book. They are just a start!

GENERAL INFORMATION

BOOKS
These books all present a large number of inventions of all different kinds:
Oxford Illustrated Encyclopedia of Invention and Technology edited by Sir Monty Finniston (Oxford University Press, 1992)
Usborne Illustrated Handbook of Invention and Discovery by Struan Reid (Usborne, 1986)
Invention by Lionel Bender (Dorling Kindersley, 1986)
The Way Things Work by David Macaulay (Dorling Kindersley, 1988)
Key Moments in Science and Technology by Keith Wicks (Hamlyn, 1999)
A History of Invention by Trevor I. Williams (Little Brown, 1999)

WEBSITE
For information on many different inventions, visit:
http://inventors.about.com

MUSEUMS
Many large museums contain interesting artefacts related to people of the past, and some have collections that may be more specifically about some of the themes covered in this book.

To find out more about the museums in your area, ask in your local library or tourist information office, or look in the telephone directory.

A useful guide is *Museums & Galleries in Great Britain & Ireland* (British Leisure Publications, East Grinstead) which tells you about over 1,300 places to visit. For a good introduction to the subjects covered in this book, visit:

Science Museum, Exhibition Road, London SW7
www.sciencemuseum.org.uk

For displays and information about many of the earliest ideas and inventions, go to:

British Museum, Great Russell Street, London WC1
www.britishmuseum.co.uk

SHIPS & NAVIGATION

BOOKS
Cargo Ships by Althea and Edward Parker (A & C Black, 1992)

MUSEUMS
National Maritime Museum, Romney Road, Greenwich, London SE10
www.nmm.ac.uk

SITES
Many of Britain's ports have interesting museums or old ships that you can visit. Here are a few of the most famous:
Mary Rose and HMS **Victory**, HM Naval Base, Portsmouth, Hampshire
www.maryrose.org
Cutty Sark, Greenwich Pier, London SE10.
The fastest clipper ever built.
www.cuttysark.org.uk
SS Great Britain, Great Western Dock, Gas Ferry Road, Bristol, Avon
Brunel's famous ship, the first ocean-going vessel to be built of iron.
www.ss-great-britain.com

AEROPLANES

BOOKS
Flying Machine by Andrew Nahum (Dorling Kindersley, 1990)
Flight and Flying Machines by Steve Parker (Dorling Kindersley, 1990)

MUSEUMS
Look out for demonstrations of old aeroplanes flying. You can visit the Science Museum, London (address above), or:
Imperial War Museum, Lambeth Road, London, SE1
www.iwm.org.uk
Imperial War Museum, Duxford Airfield, Duxford, Cambridgeshire

The Shuttleworth Collection, Old Warden, near Biggleswade, Bedfordshire
www.shuttleworth.org

Museum of Flight, East Fortune Airfield, nr North Berwick, Lothian
www.north-berwick.co.uk

SPACE

MUSEUMS
One of the best space travel exhibitions is at the **Science Museum**, London (address above).

BOOKS
The Newsround Book of Space by Nick Heathcote, Marshall Corwin and Susie Staples (BBC Books, 1993)

INDEX

INDEX